Stages of Perseverance

Marlon Stovall AKA Rocky

Copyright © 2018 Marlon Stovall Aka Rocky

All rights reserved.

ISBN: 1727346556
ISBN-13: 9781727346558

DEDICATION

This book is dedicated to all the underdogs that are trying to find their place in the world and aspiring to have a voice! We all know 'Life Isn't Easy' but we must persevere through lives struggles. When we endure this thing we call LIFE we become stronger individuals. This book is for the people who have persevered triumphs and tribulations in life from love, pain and even enduring insecurities. This book is for the readers to relate and understand they are not alone. I have persevered through so much in life with self-esteem issues, anger, hurt, desiring love and some of my personal demons and even self-acceptance and it makes me the warrior I am today and I want to inspire others to never give up. Remember we are not perfect but we all are in the process of progression.

CONTENTS

        Acknowledgments   i

1. *Perseverance*
2. *CockySwagg*
3. *Broken Images of Picture Perfect*
4. *IDRC*
5. *Dear Rum*
6. *As You Will*
7. *Loved But Estranged*
8. *Is My Disability Truly My Downfall*
9. *Diss-Ability*
10. *ColdHeart Massacre*

Exclusive Bonus Poems

11. Arsenic

12. Colossal Strength

ACKNOWLEDGMENTS

    I want to first thank every person who has supported me from the beginning. I want to thank my mother Essie Stovall for pushing me to use my talent to help others , my best friends' Cherry Austin and Quincy Keith, Nicole Bradley and Deniece James , and one of my favorite patients from my job , Ms. Carol Lambert for speaking life into writing another book even though there was times I struggled to keep motivated. I want to thank my supporters that went out there way to purchase my first book and hoping you guys love this book. Last but surely not the least; I want to thank God for giving me the gifting me with many talents. When God gives you a talent you use your gift to bless others. I want to extend a very special shout out to one of my college teachers, and mentor " Dr.Paul Brinker " for speaking life over me in college when I felt like giving up.
    He spoke these words in the hardest of times ,"Stovall your story is Perseverance". You inspired the title of my second book!

    Peace and Blessings,

    Marlon Stovall

<u>Perseverance</u>

Don't you ever wonder , how the hell am I still here!!? When I have been through enough shit; been dragged in and out ; thrown around, felt stabbed into the ground ; Because their inability to see the greatness within me. Some just won't let you be great! If you rising above its so much received hate! Building Strength in the hardest of times, speechless, felt worthless but never giving up! How Am I still standing when I been knocked down , my pride stolen from me. Struggled with self-esteem , stripped me to nothing! But there is a beast waiting deep inside of me wantin to roar. The haters thought I will stand here weeping long , feeling unsure. Perseverance is a piece of gold waiting to be shaped into a solid coin! I have a Professor in college telling me that my story is Perseverance, when I felt worthless, so worried about being liked, had my dream in my hand and then just that fast it disappeared out my sight. I had to put up a fight! I eventually pop back up full of stress but use it as fuel to regain my resilient copper skin! I have to believe in me, when nobody else didn't see my greatness! I am an ostracized citizen , dealing with bitches that made me feel like less of a human. Admit my disabilities, live in my truth! My family's blood run through my vains and having to find myself in my roots. Mama always said as a child , I never took "NO" for an answer! Stubborn because I didn't choose to stick to people's standards. I am a MAN first of my own individuality. I always wanted to fit in with the normal folks, but wasn't made with the same ropes. My Pops raised no punk , sisters pushed me when my mind was stuck in a funk. I Know I am Capable of anything…. I can put my mind to but because of my lesser strengths people underestimate you. Can't nobody be a better version of me , So I choose to live in my truth!

<u>CockySwagg</u>

Dez normal wannabes have the audacity to stick their heads up and sneeze bcuz dey luk down on peeps with disabilities! So what!? They hate on us because their ignorant minds limits us plus love to hate on our capabilities, See we are like magic, what's happenin is that we make the world go round. Wake Up! Wake Up Today! We fight society every damn day and We didn't come to play! So many try to tell me what I can and ...can't, I didn't take no for answers

,stayed LIT like a lamp , foreva my light shine , In the 21st century it's our time! No I'm not slow , on the short yellow bus I use to go, was bullied for it , Sand thrown in my afro for being different, so I had to go harda, to have something to show for it! This a clap back for the ones who look down up on me! Hated on me because with God he gave me victory to have the ability to be mighty. See I hated as a kid , how kids played me for stupid. At a certain age got time for the shitz! Left me behind, because hangin with them in certain crowds was a crime. I guess I didn't move too fast for the labeled *"normal"*. Remember feeling down because inside I felt so low, but I never let my light blow! See people not aware of their able body privilege, some so shallow they look at us and can't handle it. I guess we not popular, so the fuck what, do you, like they do. Trying to fit it in , doesn't create wins. Be yourself and never hold back the real you

Broken Images of Picture Perfect

I am not perfect, to you I made you feel cheated. You made me feel incompleted. It's not any amount of loneliness that will ever make me get back with you. Embarrass me in front of friends because your insecurities ran deep and through. I'm lost for words and stuck on stupid because I just ran out of options on what to do. I can say now you kept me sunked in a bad place , as I battled depression of my new life , YOU was just waiting for your turn to utilize the knife. Outside others said we looked like we was happy but behind closed doors I was trapped in complete misery . Dammit I ask myself now why did I stay when you made feel some type of way. See if it was the old me I would've busted you in your ass because of the games you played. Turning 360 ; a nightmare and I can say I was stupid to even allow myself to let it get this far. You always was leaving cuts deeps in me creating new scars. But I finally built that courage to push you out my life because you was stunting my growth. You pulling me one way, constantly being manipulative and dug me to my lowest of lows. No I didn't give you the picture perfect but the times I gave my heart you belittle everything about me. You don't love me I guess I find it elsewhere. THE HEAT is hot and the tension is a flare. The light is slowing down coming to my vision and clearing the glare. So now it's time to tell you to get the fuck out of here.

IDRC-I Don't Really Care

You know what!? I do enough to feed the needy if I have to ; but I give too much of myself! Overexerted I have become! The users drain me. Dealing with friends that are straight up flaky! If I react they think I'm tripping like a spoiled baby. But do they forget how much I have done for them? From giving all fibers of my being. 9 times out of ten I give myself generously! I just don't know what they seeing? Hmph they must be blind and think I have the time for unnecessary. Always think I'm scary, never afraid to speak my mind! I over extend my shine to mankind, and people think it's sweet and fine. See I finally have a voice! People will turn your volume down just to turn themselves. Thinking you always must agree, and be open hearted and free. I extend enough of my generosity. Does it strike your curiosity how I give my heart free and the actions you returned with "X" excluding me! I love hard, and yet still have my guard because you hurt me, I block the boomerang with elbow and knee. I'm tired of letting you get to me. Trying to change that side of me. Fueling the fire to ignite a scene. I shouldn't have to keep it cute and keep it clean. You should respect the fact I'm giving and will forever be. Now RESPECT Me!

DEAR RUM

YOU MY FRIEND HAD COMFORTED ME AT THE MOST UNCOMFORTABLE TIMES. WHEN I DIDN'T FEEL THE LOVE AT THE TIMES, YOU HELD ME TIGHT AT MY HEART. YOU SOOTHED ME WHEN I WAS HURT BY MY OWN FAMILY, AND FRIENDS AND LOVERS. OTHERS SAY "YOU JUST AN ALCOHOLIC", CARRIED AWAY I MUST ADMIT. BUT HAVE YOU FELT THE PAIN WITHIN REJECTION. THE PAIN OF BEING USED, LIKE HORRIBLE INJECTIONS. FIGHTING FOR EVERYTHING YOU WANT AND NOW IT DISAPPEARS LIKE IMAGINATIONS. I KNOW YOU NOT GOOD, YOU DON'T MEAN ME NOT A BIT OF GOOD! BUT I HAVE FELT YOU WON'T JUDGE ME WHEN I CRY BEHIND CLOSED DOORS. YOU WONT MAKE ME FEEL LIKE MY FEELINGS ARE IGNORED. YOU WON'T LEAVE ME OUT. GRANTED YOU MAY SAY THINGS YOU KNOW BETTER THAN SAYING OR NEED THE ENCOURAGEMENT TO SPEAK YOUR MIND. THAT'S BECAUSE YOU FELT LIKE YOUR WORDS ARE NOT VALUED. EVERYBODY WILL PIN POINT YOU LIKE THEY KNOW YOU WHEN IT'S ALL ASSUMPTIONS. BUT YOU SEEM TO LISTEN TO ME EVEN THOUGH IT'S JUST ME AND YOU IN MY HEAD. WHEN I HAD NO TRUE FRIENDS, DIDN'T HAVE THAT SECURITY FROM MY LOVER, YOU WERE THE ONE TO HELP ME WHEN I NEED COVER. THE WORLD SAYS "YOU DON'T NEED RUM JUST DIVORCE HER". BUT THE

MARRIAGE AND THE BOND WE GREW, JUST MAKES ME WANT THE SCENT. PEOPLE THINK THEY KNOW MY STORY BUT SHE KNOWS ME MORE.

AS YOU WILL

YOU NEVER BELIEVED IN US AS IT WAS ONLY ME IN THE BEGINNING TRYING TO LIFT YOU UP. I LIFT YOU UP AND YOU BRING ME DOWN. CONSTANT SPINNING IN CIRCLES LIKE A NONSTOP MARRY GO ROUND. INCONSISTENT IN YOUR COMMUNICATION , AS I AM REACHING OUT TO YOU THERE IS NO MUTTER OR SOUND. I AM GIVING YOU MORE THAN I SHOULD GIVE, AND MY FRIENDS TOLD ME I   HAVE BUT IN MY HEAD I WANT TO MAKE YOU MY BETTER HALF. LOOKING PAST YOUR FLAWS AND ALL. BUT YOU KEEP PULLING PLUGS , PLAYING YOUR CHARADES, AND I AM HEADED IN A DIFFERENT WAY. SO AS YOU WILL , KEEP THAT SAME ENERGY. I NEED TO TELL MYSELF TO NOT CHASE YOU BECAUSE THAT'S MISERY AND LOSING MY SERENITY. I WANT A QUIET THUNDERSTORM BUT YOU WAS TO CAUSE RIFFS IN DROWNING DEEP OCEANS , I CANT MAKE YOU FALL IN LOVE , ITS NOT A DRUG OR A

POTION TO GET YOU TO DIGEST, JUST AIR AND DUST. WHY AM I FOOLING MYSELF OVER YOU, WHEN I SHOULD'VE FOLLOWED YOUR ACTIONS AND WHAT YOU DO. AS YOU WILL , AS YOU WILL LEAVE ME BE AS YOU ARE. TOO FAR TO EVEN BE REACHED! SO WHY AM I PUSHING SO HARD???

<u>Loved But Estranged</u>

I admit in my teenage years I never understood your ways. Be hard, tough but lack the compassionate components to a potential wonderful individual. Upbringing was strict but I could not live free. I needed that time to find me and still I am. Can you imagine love without communication. Love without the sense of understanding each other. Love without the direct I love yous. Been taught that its shown in action but at the time I was yearning for deeper interactions. Love you hard when I had been verbally torn. But I have to be happy for me and live for me. Constant flashback of those moments was causing resentment. Between us there was no true settlement. In years, I have seen improvement and I see the growth in you. Taught me to work hard and get my education. In that was fueled out frustrations because I wanted to prove to you I could be somebody regardless of how I live. Eventually moved out to get my own crib. I am my own individual but those times also created an anger in me. I could never be the true person, I wanted you to see me and still hurts my deeply. I guess I wouldn't been praised better if I was a criminal but I guess to you I was living the worst. I couldn't live my life through you, I had to live for me and think of myself first. At the same time you not a horrible person. In your times I guess it was caused for reasons. But now it doesn't matter life is short and I choose love for the season.

IS MY DISABILITY TRULY MY DOWNFALL

THOUGHTS IN THE IDLE MIND TAKES OVER ME WHEN I START THINKING ABOUT THE MANY USERS IN MY LIFE. LEARNING TO HEAL ON

YOUR OWN WHILE TRYING TO REMOVE THE KNIFE. RECIPROCATION BECOMES LESS AND YOU KNOW THAT YOU ARE ACCOMPLISHED BUT YOU WONDER WHY YOU NOT RECEIVING THAT SAME LOVE THAT YOU GIVE. PEOPLE DON'T UNDERSTAND BEING DEALT THIS LIFE AND MADE ME BE THE PERSON THAT IS SO LOVING. I KNOW, I KNOW BECAUSE OF MY DISABILITY PEOPLE MUST HAVE THIS PERCEPTION THAT I AM WEAK. I LOVE HARD ON FRIENDS THAT HAVEN'T EARN MY HARD LOVE. INSTEAD I PUT ON MY ARMOR AND MY BOXING GLOVES. I FOUGHT FOR MY PEACE OF MIND AND CAN'T LET IT BE TAKEN FROM ME. BUT YOU SEE THIS LIFE GETS LONELY. SEEING THE OTHERS MOVE FASTER AND TREAT YOU LIKE YOU ARE SLOWING THEM DOWN. I WONDER WOULD PUT CONSIDER WALKING A MILE IN MY SHOES. DEFINITELY NOT BECAUSE COMMON SENSE DOESN'T COME FROM FOOLS. I HAVE TO SET MYSELF FROM OTHERS BECAUSE EVERYBODY CAN'T BE TRUSTED AND THE PREY ON ME IS WHAT THEY CHOOSE. I AM NOT FEELING SORRY FOR MYSELF OR TRYING TO GIVE BAD NEWS. BUT IF YOU LIVED MY LIFE WHAT WOULD YOU DO?

DISS-ABILITY

Tired of being in that box with everything you do is because of your disability. "Oh he can't run because of his disability", "he can't do this because he disabled! "Well wake the fuck up PEOPLE! Its always been my own people , that will tear me down. Trying to understand that the uneducated means well, but to not want to learn about someone different is the ultimate fail! The lack of understanding a person that's different and put you in the box! Yall can suck my cock-i-ness! Just don't know I am blessed , I confess this was part of my self-esteem issues but I have to realize I'm the shit! These people just don't know whom they effin with! I been the butt of the jokes, "hey he a cripple", hollllllddd up people crippled means …. YOU KNOW WHAT…(I rather not).. I aint got the time! To be fly like me is a crime! Disability in the highest of my prime! They want to throw us away! They think we have no thoughts and we're just vegetables to them bitches , they think all we do is collect government checks and lay. Lemme tell you how I bust my ass everyday! Got two college degrees, yes that's an education, and work , harder than they. And these fats, ugly, evil, unattractive people just pass us up like we can't slay. I am here just to say, don't diss-my abilities! My

Marlon Stovall Aka Rocky

community didn't come to play!

COLDHEART MASSACRE

CARRYING MY HEART IN MY HANDS, IT PULSATES AND PUMPS BLOODS ,DECREASING BECAUSE ITS TRYING TO SURVIVE. ITS ON ITS LAST OF LIFE. I AM HAVE REMOVED THE KNIVES, FROM THE MULTIPLE CHANCES I GIVEN. BEING SO DRIVEN TO BE IN LOVE AND NOT BE THAT PERSON TO GIVE UP. BUT ITS ALL TOOK A TURN NOW! NOT A CARE FOUND AND ITS GROWING COLD AT NIGHT. YOU MADE LOVE TO MY HEART AND LEFT LIKE IT WAS YOUR LAST FLIGHT. TINMAN EMPTY, NOTHING TO FORCE IT TO KEEP IT TOGETHER JUST BLEEDING. MY HEART HAS EYES AND ITS WEEPING. DAMMIT WHY DO I HAVE TO BE THAT HOPELESS ROMANTIC AND KEEP GOING AFTER THAT FANTASY THAT I BEEN DREAMING. ERASE MY MEMORIES THAT I CAN NO LONGER HAVE SOMETHING TO REFERENCE TO. BLAME THE ONE BEFORE ME WHEN I GET COLD , I USE TO JUST FALL HARD, LOVE HARD BUT ITS BEEN GIVEN TO TROLLS. MY HEART HAS BECOME COLDER THAN THE NORTHPOLE. NO STAY

AWAY FROM ME I MAY BE DANGEROUS. SEE I HAVE GIVEN MY HEART SO MUCH THAT I AM ON THE EDGE OF BEING FURIOUS NOT DELIRIOUS. AS I AM FEELING CLOSED IN MY THE COMFORT OF MY PAIN, MY HEAD SAYS BE A SAVAGE BUT I AM TOO GOOD OF A PERSON; I CAN'T TAKE ADVANTAGE. HURT PEOPLE HURT OTHER PEOPLE ;AND I DON'T WANT TO BE THE MONSTER. TRAPPED IN A IGLOO, BECAUSE IT WAS YOU THAT LEFT IT AND NEVER WAS A LATER OR A SOON. THERE WAS NO RETURN FOR YOU TO MAKE THINGS RIGHT. YOU GOT ME COLD AND MURDERED MY HEART. NOW I AM LEFT BY MYSELF PICKING UP MY PARTS.

ARSENIC

PURE HATRED, WE CAN'T EVEN BE AROUND EACH OTHER. NOPE DON'T SAY SHIT TO ME DON'T EVEN BOTHER. YOU SAID WHAT YOU SAID TO ME AND YOU MEANT EVERY VERBALLY ABUSIVE THING YOU SAID! TOXICITY WILL KILL YOUR INNER STRENGTH MAKE YOU FEEL LIKE YOU ARE NOTHING. DID I ASK TO DRINK THIS POISON? YOU MEANT TO KILL ME, THAT UNIQUE PERSON I AM NOW, YOU SPILLED YOUR ARSENIC, TRYING TO FIND A WAY TO END MY REPUTATION. WE BOTH RAN OUT OF SOLUTIONS. AT THIS POINT THIS IS WAR NOT LOVE. THERE ARE MINIMAL RESOLUTIONS. I

CAN'T DO YOU, I WANT YOU DRIFTED AWAY, DON'T CALL OUT FOR ME. IM NOT SAVING YOU! WHEN I NEEDED YOU WITH OPEN WARM ARMS WHAT HAVE YOU DONE TO HELP ME ?! RAISE ME UP TO MY CAPABILITIES TO MY BEST BEING. MALICIOUS POISON, BURNS MY LIPS , NO LONGER STRIVING FOR YOUR LOVE. I SHOULD'VE NEVER INDULGED IN YOUR POISON BECAUSE IM SINKING IN WATER ABOVE MY NECK, IM JUST TRYING TO STAY FLOATING ABOVE.

COLOSSAL STRENGTH

WHO WOULD'VE THOUGHT, AT THIS MOMENT HE BUILD A STRONG INDIVIDUAL LIKE ME? I GREW STRENGTH OF A ROCK, I'M THE SURVIVAL OF THE FITTEST AND HERE I AM KILLING IT. HE MADE ME A WARRIOR AND CREATED A FIT. IF HE CAN BUILD YOU UP, HE CAN BUILD ALL OF US! NO JELLY BACK, HIS STRENGTH GIVEN TO US NEVER SLACK. DEEP INSIDE IF YOU BELIEVE IN HIM. HE WILL TAKE YOUR EDGES AND CREATE A BEAUTIFUL IMAGE WITH A FEW TRIMS. I AM COLOSSAL AND YOU CAN BE TOO IF YOU KNOW EVERYTHING I BEEN THROUGH. I CAN STAND THROUGH ANY STORM OF THE NORM!

ABOUT THE AUTHOR

Marlon Stovall is an young individual from the Southwest Suburbs of Chicago that has introduced you to his debut poetry book "Trapped In A Thing We Call Love" has now given you "Stages of Perseverance". This book reveals the growth after heart break, overcoming disparity and insecurities, Living with a disability called Spinabifida has taught him hard lessons but also how to build tough skin; fighting for the rights of people with disabilities while educating others that we are people as well in a very sarcastic way. He feels if he can overcome struggles than every individual on this planet can do the same. Overcoming depression, feeling inadequate, finding someone to accept our flaws is what we as humans have in common.

www.ingramcontent.com/pod-product-compliance
Lightning Source LLC
Chambersburg PA
CBHW040056250526
45473CB00042B/2795